THIS LAND CALLED AMERICA: NORTH DAKOTA

CREATIVE EDUCATION

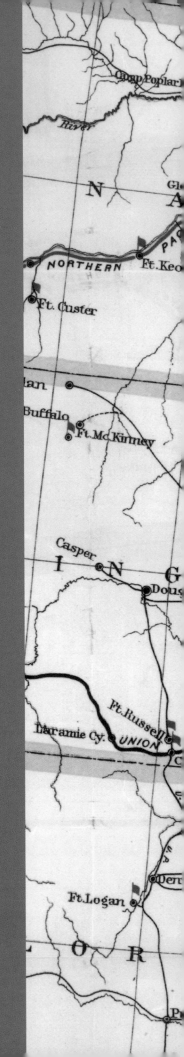

Published by Creative Education
P.O. Box 227, Mankato, Minnesota 56002
Creative Education is an imprint of The Creative Company
www.thecreativecompany.us

Design by Blue Design (www.bluedes.com)
Art direction by Rita Marshall
Book production by The Design Lab
Printed in the United States of America

Photographs by Alamy (All Canada Photos, Richard Cummins, David R. Frazier
Photolibrary, Inc., Danita Delimont, Jason Lindsey, Royal Geographical Society,
Tom Till, Worldwide Picture Library), Corbis (Tom Bean, Annie Griffiths Belt,
Bettmann, Lowell Georgia, Layne Kennedy, PoodlesRock, Richard Hamilton
Smith, Smithsonian Institution), Getty Images (Willard Clay, Daniel J Cox,
Jeff Foott), Minden Pictures (Tim Fitzharris)

Library of Congress Cataloging-in-Publication Data
Peterson, Sheryl.
North Dakota / by Sheryl Peterson.
p. cm. — (This land called America)
Includes bibliographical references and index.
ISBN 978-1-58341-787-4
1. North Dakota—Juvenile literature. I. Title. II. Series.
F636.3.P48 2009
978.4—dc22   2008009516

First Edition
9 8 7 6 5 4 3 2 1

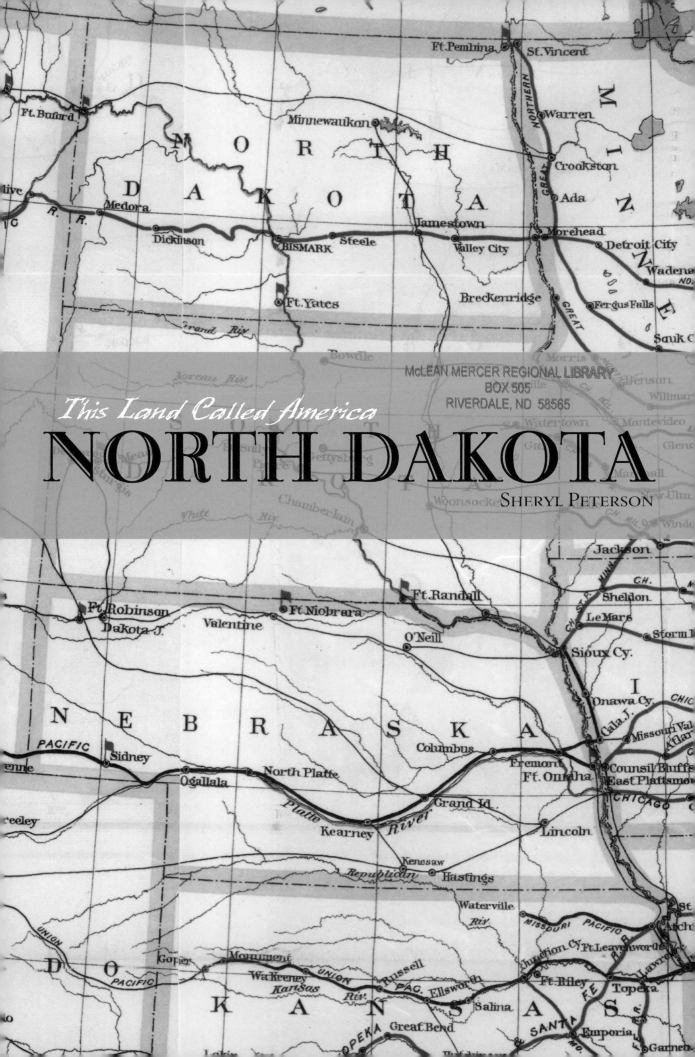

This Land Called America

NORTH DAKOTA

SHERYL PETERSON

North Dakota

SHERYL PETERSON

At daybreak, riders saddle up their horses. They are ready to be North Dakota cowboys for the day. *Giddy-up!* The riders follow the well-worn, cross-country trails. They trot across grassy prairie land. They amble over flat river-bottom country. Purple thistle and yarrow dot the plains. Cottonwood leaves provide a splash of yellow along the creek banks. The riders pull their horses to a stop. They peer at the strange rock formations of the Badlands and watch mule deer and wild turkeys in the distance. At day's end, the cowboys head back to the ranch. Around a cozy campfire, they relax and marvel at the star-filled North Dakota sky.

YEAR

1682 French explorer René-Robert de La Salle claims North Dakota for France.

EVENT

Gateway to the Old West

IN THE EARLY DAYS, NORTH DAKOTA WAS HOME TO SEVERAL AMERICAN INDIAN TRIBES. THE LAKOTA AND NAKOTA SIOUX LIVED IN THE SOUTHEASTERN PART OF THE STATE. THE SIOUX HUNTED BUFFALO AND USED THE ANIMALS FOR FOOD AND CLOTHING. THEY BUILT TEPEES, OR TENTS, BY COVERING POLES WITH BUFFALO HIDE. THE TEPEES COULD BE TAKEN DOWN AND MOVED EASILY TO NEW HUNTING GROUNDS.

Other Indian groups lived in settled villages. The Mandan Indians built round earthen lodges along the Missouri River. Several families lived in each lodge, with their cooking fires in the center. The Chippewa and Cree lived in the northeastern part of North Dakota.

In 1682, René-Robert de La Salle claimed North Dakota and much of the land east of the Mississippi River for France. He named the area Louisiana after King Louis XIV of France. More than 50 years later, a French-Canadian named Pierre de La Vérendrye entered the region. French-Canadian fur traders began setting up trading posts in North Dakota.

American Indians who lived on the plains in teepees (opposite) used hides from animals such as buffalo and elk to make clothes (above).

YEAR
1738 Pierre de La Vérendrye leads the first known European-American expedition into North Dakota.
EVENT

- 7 -

1803   The U.S. gains most of North Dakota from France through the Louisiana Purchase.

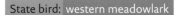

In 1803, United States president Thomas Jefferson made a land deal with France. It was called the Louisiana Purchase. Much of North Dakota became part of the U.S. at that time. Jefferson sent explorers Meriwether Lewis and William Clark to map out the region and find a route to the Pacific Ocean. Lewis and Clark left St. Louis, Missouri, and traveled up the Missouri River.

After crossing South Dakota, the explorers canoed into North Dakota. Lewis and Clark spent more time in North Dakota than in any other place they visited. Their group built Fort Mandan by the Missouri River near Stanton. They met Sacagawea, a young Shoshone Indian woman. She joined the expedition, along with her husband, who was an interpreter. Sacagawea helped Lewis and Clark get horses and showed them the best places to cross the mountains as they traveled west.

In 1861, the Dakota Territory was created. This included most of North and South Dakota. Soon after, the U.S. government passed the Homestead Act, which allowed pioneers to work the land they claimed for five years, and then they could own it. Some people started ranches and grazed cattle on the prairie. Others raised wheat in the Red River Valley.

Life was not easy for the pioneers. Winters were long and harsh. Blizzards blew furiously across the Dakota plains.

The guidance of Sacagawea (center, opposite) helped Lewis and Clark on their expedition through the West.

In the 1880s, North Dakota settlers relied on trains in towns such as Mandan to bring much-needed supplies.

As more settlers claimed land, the American Indians lost their hunting grounds. They were moved by the U.S. government onto reservations, or areas of land that were set aside for them.

The U.S. government made treaties, or agreements, with the Indians to give them food and supplies. But soon the treaties were forgotten. For years, Sioux chief Sitting Bull led his people in battle against the U.S. Army in attempts to save native lands. Finally, in 1881, Sitting Bull surrendered at Fort Buford, near Williston.

On November 2, 1889, North and South Dakota became two separate states. North Dakota became well known for its farms, and the early 1900s were prosperous times. The Northern Pacific Railway sold land to rich businessmen. They started huge wheat farms called "bonanza farms." The most modern planting and harvesting machinery was used on these farms. However, the demand for land forced bonanza farm owners to sell out to smaller farmers. A wave of new settlers arrived, hoping to work the land, and by 1920, the state's population had reached nearly 650,000.

YEAR

1804 Meriwether Lewis and William Clark begin to explore the region that is now North Dakota.

EVENT

After he surrendered, Sitting Bull lived for a time on the Standing Rock reservation in South Dakota.

Badlands and Farmlands

THE MIDWESTERN STATE OF NORTH DAKOTA IS SHAPED LIKE A RECTANGLE. NORTH DAKOTA SHARES BORDERS WITH CANADA TO THE NORTH, SOUTH DAKOTA TO THE SOUTH, MINNESOTA TO THE EAST, AND MONTANA TO THE WEST. NORTH DAKOTA IS LOCATED IN THE CENTER OF THE NORTH AMERICAN CONTINENT. A STONE PYRAMID MARKS THE EXACT SPOT IN THE NORTHERN CITY OF RUGBY.

Many years ago, huge sheets of ice called glaciers covered eastern North Dakota. When they melted, the glaciers formed lakes, hills, and rich farmland. North Dakota's only forests lie in the northern Turtle Mountains. Moose, ruffed grouse, and snowy owls make their homes there.

Snowy owls live mainly in the Arctic Circle, but some are found as far south as North Dakota.

Western North Dakota is part of the Missouri Plateau. The Missouri River winds through this area. The Plateau is part of the Great Plains region of North America, which stretches from Canada to Texas. Sheep and cattle graze on the Plateau's hardy wheatgrass. Canada geese, ducks, and herons nest in the region's wetlands.

The North Dakota Badlands are in the western part of the state. The Badlands were formed when wind and water carved out rolling hills and buttes. A butte is a flat-topped hill with steep sides. White Butte is North Dakota's highest point, at 3,506 feet (1,069 m) above sea level.

The plains of North Dakota are the perfect place to plant fields of durum wheat.

YEAR
1812   Pembina, in the northeastern corner of North Dakota, is established as the area's first settlement.
EVENT

Prickly pear cactus, sagebrush, and wildflowers dot the Badlands. Wild buffalo, elk, deer, and coyotes roam the land. More than 180 species of birds fly overhead. Wild horses run free in the Painted Canyon, located seven miles (11 km) east of Medora.

North Dakota has many rivers but few lakes. The Sheyenne River empties into the Red River of the North. West of the Red River Valley are the James and Souris rivers. The Missouri River starts in Montana and flows across North Dakota. The river is nicknamed "Big Muddy" because of all the dirt it carries.

Devil's Lake, in the east, is the largest natural lake in North Dakota. Dams on rivers form other large lakes such as Lake

---

Mule deer (above) can be found near the rocky valley where the Little Missouri River—which begins in North Dakota—feeds into the "Big Muddy" (opposite).

1861 The U.S. Congress creates the Dakota Territory, which is the northernmost part of the Louisiana Purchase.

Sakakawea. This lake was created by the Garrison Dam on the Missouri River. It is 178 miles (287 km) long and stretches almost to the Montana border. Fishermen catch trout, Chinook salmon, and walleye in the state's waterways.

Sunflowers are grown for their seeds, which can be eaten by people and animals or made into oil.

North Dakota produces most of the world's durum wheat, which is a hardy wheat used mainly for making pasta. Large fields of wheat are planted in the spring and harvested in the fall before the ground freezes. North Dakota produces more sunflowers, honey, and navy beans than any other state. Farmers also grow a large portion of the world's corn and sugar beets.

Western North Dakota is rich in natural resources such as oil and lignite coal. Oil is drilled for in the Williston Basin. It is North Dakota's main mining product. The state's land also yields stores of sand, gravel, and clay.

In the fall, North Dakota farmers are busy harvesting their large fields of wheat.

North Dakota has warm summers and long, cold winters. Gusty blizzards blow snow across the flat prairie from November to March. Central North Dakota has an average rainfall of 22 inches (55 m) a year. But in April 1997, melting snows caused the Red River to flood, leaving thousands of people in Grand Forks homeless. The drier western part of the state receives fewer than 16 inches (40 cm) of rain each year.

YEAR

1872 Tracks for the Northern Pacific Railway are built over the Red River, and the first train crosses into Fargo.

EVENT

Northern Friends

North Dakota's name comes from the Dakota Indian word for friend. Many immigrants moved to the friendly state from Norway, Sweden, Germany, and England. Today, most North Dakotans are of northern European descent. Fewer than 10 percent of the state's residents are American Indian, African American, Asian American, or Hispanic.

Overall, North Dakota does not have many people. Only the states of Vermont and Wyoming have smaller populations. However, North Dakota has more churches for its population than any other U.S. state. Most of these churches are either Lutheran or Roman Catholic.

Churches were built in the middle of farmland in North Dakota so that rural families would not have to travel far.

Today, most of North Dakota's people live in the Red River Valley. Fargo, the state's largest city, lies along the Red River. So does Grand Forks, the third-largest city.

Bismarck was a sleepy railroad town in the 1870s, but by 1889, it was the state capital.

In the early days, most pioneers came to North Dakota to find rich farming and grazing land. In 1883, the Marquis de Mores came to the city of Missouri, North Dakota, from

YEAR

1888   A January storm called "The School Children's Blizzard" claims the lives of many children as they leave school.

EVENT

- *19* -

Theodore Roosevelt (above) built his first cabin at the Maltese Cross (opposite) during the winter of 1883–84.

France and built a meat-packing plant. Dakotans called him "the crazy Frenchman." De Mores started his own town on the opposite bank of the Missouri River. He named the town Medora after his wife. He also built a 26-room summer house called the Chateau de Mores that overlooks the town.

One of the Marquis' occasional neighbors was Theodore "Teddy" Roosevelt. Roosevelt first visited North Dakota's Badlands in 1883. He liked adventure and thought the fresh air would help his asthma. Roosevelt set up two cattle ranches: the Maltese Cross and the Elkhorn Ranch. After hunting buffalo and working as a cowboy throughout the 1880s, Roosevelt was healthier and more energetic than he had ever been. He went on to serve as the 26th president of the U.S from 1901 to 1909. "I would not have been president had it not been for my experience in North Dakota," Roosevelt said later.

North Dakota has produced other well-known Americans, too. Louis L'Amour was a popular writer who was born in Jamestown in 1908. L'Amour wrote more than 100 books about the West. His books include *Hondo, How the West Was Won,* and *Ride the River.*

YEAR

1889 North Dakota becomes the 39th state on November 2.

EVENT

Lawrence Welk was a famous American musician from North Dakota. Welk was born in Strasburg in 1903. His family immigrated to the U.S. from Germany and was made up of poor farmers. Welk worked long hours on the farm to buy his first instrument, an accordion. Later, he was the popular host of *The Lawrence Welk Show* from 1951 to 1982.

Today, many North Dakotans farm or raise cattle. They also raise hogs, turkeys, and honeybees. Farmers grow barley, wheat, and sunflower seeds. The world's largest sunflower oil plant is located in Enderlin. Many people work in food processing plants that produce bread, frozen potatoes, vegetable oil, and pasta.

Farmers may divide their wheat fields in different patterns (above), but all are harvested the same basic way (opposite).

YEAR

1915

EVENT

Farmer Charles Townley forms the Nonpartisan League to help farmers gain a voice in governmental policies.

North Dakota cowboy

In 1951, oil was discovered in the northwestern Williston Basin near the town of Tioga. Today, the oil industry is still booming. New technology and high oil prices create good-paying jobs for many North Dakotans. North Dakotans are skilled factory workers, too. They make farm machinery, tools, and aircraft parts.

North Dakota has a low crime rate and is one of the safest places to live in the U.S. From agriculture to quality of life, the state of North Dakota is at the top of the charts.

Along with cowboys (above), oil drilling rigs (above and opposite) are a common sight in western North Dakota, an area that has large oil reserves about two miles (3.2 km) below ground.

YEAR

1947 Theodore Roosevelt National Memorial Park is established in the Badlands, becoming a national park in 1978.

EVENT

Land of Natural Beauty

NORTH DAKOTA IS CALLED "THE PEACE GARDEN STATE."
THE INTERNATIONAL PEACE GARDEN LIES IN THE TURTLE
MOUNTAINS OF NORTH DAKOTA AND CANADA. IT IS A
SYMBOL OF FRIENDSHIP BETWEEN THE U.S. AND CANADA.
FOUNTAINS, TREES, AND A HUGE CLOCK MADE OF REAL
FLOWERS DECORATE THE GARDENS.

Every year, American Indians gather south of the Canadian border in the city of Bismarck for the United Tribes International Powwow. A powwow is a ceremonial day for Indian tribes. At the powwow, Indians play traditional music. People perform traditional dances that tell stories about animals and brave hunters.

The Indians who first lived in North Dakota called the west-central region "bad land." Today, people call it one of the most beautiful and mysterious places on Earth. Strange-shaped, colorful domes and towers rise up throughout the Badlands. Different minerals present in the rocks produce shades of green, yellow, and purple. There are also petrified, or hardened, trees and cone-like hills.

Theodore Roosevelt National Park is the top tourist attraction in the Badlands. The 70,446-acre (28,509 ha) park was created in 1978. It is the only national park in the U.S. named after a person. The park contains forests, bright-colored tablelands, and high buttes. The Little Missouri River runs through it. The Maah Daah Hey Trail is a hiking and biking path that connects the northern and southern units of the park. In the summer, a Western show called the *Medora Musical* is produced in Medora, near the entrance to the park.

From the International Peace Garden (opposite) to the Badlands in Theodore Roosevelt National Park (pictured), North Dakota is prized for its natural beauty.

YEAR

1953   Workers complete construction on the giant Garrison Dam on the Missouri River.

EVENT

Every fall, a huge Scandinavian festival called the Norsk Hostfest is held farther north in the city of Minot. The festival honors the state's immigrants from Norway, Sweden, Finland, Denmark, and Iceland. Visitors eat special foods from these countries. They shop for Norwegian sweaters and Finnish glass. They watch woodcarvers and even dance with trolls!

People traveling in the southern part of the state enjoy the Enchanted Highway. The 32-mile (52 km) stretch of road starts about 20 miles east of Dickinson and heads south to Regent. Along the highway are seven of the world's largest scrap metal sculptures, including *Geese in Flight*, *Deer Crossing*, and *The Tin Family*. The artist, Gary Greff, plans to create more sculptures so that people can be entertained while on long car trips.

Children and adults in North Dakota love to be outdoors. Camping, fishing, hiking, and deer hunting are popular pastimes. In the winter, people snowmobile and ice fish. But at any time of the year, North Dakotans can attend symphony orchestra concerts and tour art museums in Fargo, Minot, and Grand Forks. During the fall and winter, people have to take sides when it comes to sports. Some cheer for the University

Southeast of the Little Missouri River (above) is the Enchanted Highway, which offers metal sculptures as scenery (opposite).

YEAR

1997   Severe flooding of the Red River of the North causes serious damage to cities in the Red River Valley.

EVENT

QUICK FACTS

Population: 639,715

Largest city: Fargo (pop. 92,660)

Capital: Bismarck

Entered the union: November 2, 1889

Nickname: Peace Garden State

State flower: wild prairie rose

State bird: western meadowlark

Size: 70,700 sq mi (183,112 sq km)—19th-biggest in U.S.

Major industries: farming, ranching, mining

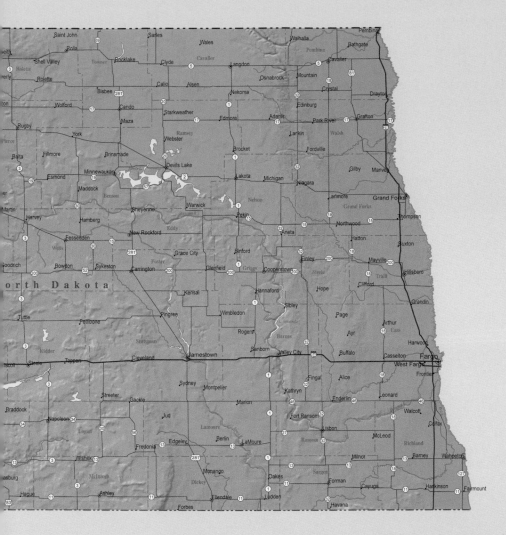

of North Dakota Fighting Sioux. Others root for the North Dakota University Bison.

Today, North Dakota's government is working to attract more young people to the state by bringing in more technology-based businesses. It hopes that a more youthful population will give North Dakota the "strength to make the future glorious," as the official state song says.

North Dakota is a land of natural beauty to all kinds of people. Its wide-open spaces seem to stretch on forever. Visitors ride on horseback across the windswept plains and gaze at the strange rock formations of the Badlands. And people who already live in North Dakota marvel, like President Roosevelt did, at their "land of vast, silent spaces."

YEAR

2007   The New Homestead Act, which would offer financial help to people relocating to North Dakota, is introduced.

EVENT

- 31 -

BIBLIOGRAPHY

Farcountry Press. "History, Maps, and Travel Information on the Lewis and Clark Trail." Traveler's Guide to the Lewis and Clark Trail. http://www.lewisandclark.com/tourismguide/index.html.

Laskin, David. *The Children's Blizzard.* New York: Harper Perennial, 2005.

Smolan, Rick, and David Cohen. *North Dakota 24/7.* New York: DK Publishing, 2004.

State of North Dakota. "State Facts." North Dakota State Government. http://www.nd.gov/category.htm?id=147.

Witteman, Barbara. *Prairie in Her Heart: Prairie Women of North Dakota.* Charleston, S.C.: Arcadia Publishing, 2001.

INDEX

DATE DUE

JUL 3 1 2010			

Demco, Inc. 38-293